DOT.COMMON SENSE

How to stay smart and safe online

Ben Hubbard

Illustrated by
Beatriz Castro

Published in paperback in Great Britain in 2019
by Wayland
Copyright © Hodder and Stoughton, 2018
All rights reserved
Editor: Sarah Peutrill
Design: Collaborate
ISBN: 978 1 5263 0572 5

Printed and bound in China

Wayland, an imprint of
Hachette Children's Group
Part of Hodder and Stoughton
Carmelite House
50 Victoria Embankment
London EC4Y 0DZ
An Hachette UK Company
www.hachette.co.uk
www.hachettechildrens.co.uk

FSC
www.fsc.org

MIX
Paper from
responsible sources
FSC® C104740

Contents

Chapter 1: Introducing the Internet

What is the Internet?

When we go online it is like we step through a window into a different world. This is the world of the Internet. Here, we can connect with friends, play games, watch films, listen to music and find information about almost anything. However, just like the real world, the Internet has its dangers. This is why **it pays to stay smart, safe and use your common sense** when you are online. This book will teach you how.

What's through here?

Sam and Olivia are brother and sister. Sometimes they explore the Internet together, but they also use it in different ways. Sam loves online games and posts photos on his social media account. Olivia looks at websites about sport and chats with her friends using instant messaging.

Digital Devices

We can use many different computer devices to go online. These include laptops, tablets, phones, games consoles and wearable computers, such as smart watches. We use these devices to send each other information over the Internet.

Online or Offline?

Being online simply means being connected to the Internet. Otherwise you are offline. We can connect to the Internet without wires using the signal from our mobile phones. We can also connect using Wi-Fi.

It's the Internet. Let's have a look.

5

The Enormous Internet

The Internet is like a series of highways that links computer devices across the world. This allows billions of people to send information to each other. The information can be sent any time and arrives in seconds. At any time of day or night you can send emails, watch a new film trailer, or play a game against someone on the other side of the planet. This makes **the Internet a fast, fun world that never sleeps**. It also unites most computer users into one giant global network.

Internet or World Wide Web?

People often think the Internet and the World Wide Web are the same thing, but they are different. **The Internet is simply a global network of computers.** The World Wide Web is made up of all the websites that are on this network. The World Wide Web is where people spend most of their time when they use the Internet.

Who Uses the Internet?

The Internet is used by many people for many different reasons. Some people use it for entertainment or to buy things. Others use it to communicate. Many people use it to learn about new subjects.

Most people use the Internet for good. But others use it for dishonest and even dangerous purposes. They may cheat or steal from people, or do them harm in other ways. This is why **we need to protect ourselves when we are online.**

Most of the information that travels around the Internet comes from websites. A website is a collection of web pages stored on a large computer, called a server. When we click on a web page, packets of information from the website are sent to our computer.

Often we don't know who is controlling a website or what part of the world it is coming from. Some websites are safe for children, others are for adults only. For this reason, **it's best to have a trusted adult around when you are visiting new websites.**

Look, a new superhero film.

And my favourite game.

Who Controls the Internet?

The Internet is not controlled by any one person, government or organisation. This also means no-one is in charge of the Internet and no-one checks what is being put there.

Olivia's Website Favourites

Many people organise the websites they visit most often into their 'Favourites' folder. Here are some of Olivia's favourites:

www.funology.com: games, recipes and jokes for bored kids.

www.bbc.co.uk/cbeebies: news, games and activities about your favourite CBBC shows.

www.ngkids.co.uk: all about the Earth, including animals, science and history.

Because of this, anyone can upload information to the Internet, even if it isn't true. Sometimes it's hard to know what is true and what is false. Either way, once information is uploaded to the Internet it can stay there forever.

The Online Real World

The Internet can feel like a far-off, invisible world that takes place behind our screens. **But it is actually closely connected to our real world.** Behind every computer device logged onto the Internet is a person controlling it. We don't know most of these people and we don't know who or what we might meet when we go online. For this reason it is important to be careful and keep our eyes open to online dangers.

WOW, the Internet is a BIG place!

Shhhhh, I'm playing my favourite game!

Digital Dangers

Here are the main dangers in the world of the Internet to watch out for. They are:

CYBER STRANGERS

Online strangers that we need to be careful of because they may not be who they say they are.

ADULT-ONLY WEBSITES

Websites with information that is unsuitable for children, or websites which show naked people.

TROLLS

Someone who says nasty things online about other people.

CYBER BULLIES

An online bully who hurts others by being mean and spreading lies.

VIRUSES AND MALWARE

Software that is designed to harm your computer.

CYBER CRIMINALS

Dishonest people that cheat and lie to make money from people online.

Awesome Internet

The Internet may have its dangers, but where would we be without it? We would have to: post real letters instead of emailing each other; talk on our landline phones instead of instant messaging; write journals about ourselves instead of using social media; read giant encyclopedias instead of googling things. The world would be a far worse place! So remember that the Internet is awesome.

Look out for more reasons why at the end of every chapter.

Chapter 2: Internet Aware
Getting Prepared

Every time you log onto the Internet it's like going on an adventure. It can take you anywhere – from coming face to face with a saltwater crocodile to choosing a new character for an online game. Although this often happens from the comfort of your chair, you will still have to be prepared.

You'll need to arm yourself with strong passwords and **common sense** and keep your personal information and online identity protected. You'll also have to look after your computer, mobile phone or tablet. And finally, you'll need a trusted adult who can help you along the way.

I'm getting prepared to be safe online.

Olivia and Sam's dad is their **trusted adult.** He is helping Sam and Olivia **get prepared and Internet aware.**

A Trusted Adult

A trusted adult is an older friend who can help you get started online and stay close during your **Internet adventure.** Your trusted adult could be a parent, guardian, older family member or a teacher at school. It's best to choose someone who knows something about the Internet, otherwise it will be you helping them!

Personal Information

Drawing up some online rules with your trusted adult is good preparation for the Internet. This means everyone will know you're safe whether you're using a smartphone or a tablet computer. You can sign the rules at the end to make it official!

These are Sam and Olivia's rules:

1. I promise to stick to these online rules!

2. I will never give out my real name, address or contact details online unless my trusted adult says it's ok.

3. I will never arrange to meet with someone I meet online, unless my parents agree.

4. I won't post photos of myself or others without my trusted adult's approval.

5. I won't download anything without first checking with my trusted adult.

6. I will tell my trusted adult if anything online makes me uncomfortable.

7. I will treat people online as I treat them in real life.

Your Online Identity

Your online identity is how you show yourself in the Internet world. It is made up of the information that you post on websites. This includes your profile on a social media account, photos that you post, and comments you make about video clips, games or books. Things that you 'like' also make up your online identity.

Creating an online identity is fun, but it's also something you need to protect. This makes sure that your real identity is never revealed.

14Spyro

Password

A username is a special nickname for being online.

My username is '14Spyro'.

Dad is helping Olivia and Sam set up their social media accounts. This involves choosing a username, a password and an avatar – an online face.

Pick an Online Face

An avatar is a picture that you use online instead of a real photo. You could choose your favourite pop star or film actor or anything you like. Choosing an avatar is great fun. You can have a different avatar for different websites and change them as often as you like.

CC-8:)

Password

My username is 'CC-8:)'.

Powerful Passwords

To keep your online information safe you need a strong password. Websites such as social media sites ask you to enter your password every time your log in. Your password needs to be easy for you to remember but hard for others to guess.

The strongest passwords use letters and numbers. But using your real name and birthday is too obvious. Instead, try numbers and words that are meaningful only to you. **Only share your password with your trusted adult and never write it down.**

Remember to always log-out when you've finished using a website.

Sam's Secret Password

(He changed it after this book was published.)

6 – The number of times Sam saw his favourite film last year.

msicO – Which spells out '**m**y **s**ister **is** **c**alled **O**livia'.

28 – Sam's favourite TV channel.

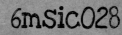

6msicO28

Keeping Personal Information Private

The world of the Internet is a massive place. It is visited by over three billion users worldwide. You know a few of these people, but **most of them are strangers.** In the real world, you wouldn't give out your personal information to strangers in the street.

The same rules apply when you are online.

How does he know who I am?

Hello Sam!

MY NAME IS SAM

12 STAPLETON ROAD

I AM 7 YEARS OLD

07870 102030

CLINTON PRIMARY SCHOOL

Your Digital Footprint

EMAILS

ONLINE GAMES

When you travel though the online world you leave behind a trail. This is called a **digital footprint.** Your digital footprint is a **record of what you have done online.** It shows what you searched for, which websites you visited, and how long you spent there.

Personal Information

Your personal information is made up of the **private details** that only your family and closest friends should know. It is dangerous to give this information out to strangers.

Your personal information includes:

Name Age

Address School

Sports or after-school clubs

Telephone numbers **Family details**

Place of birth

Town

Duh! I wonder?!

Sam and Olivia are learning that keeping personal information private is one of the most important things about being online.

Public Information

Information that is ok to make public online can include your **likes and dislikes.** Your favourite colour, singer and comic-book hero are all safe details. They do not give away anything too personal about you.

GOOGLE

ONLINE SHOPPING

FACEBOOK

TWITTER

Your digital footprint is different from your online identity because only computer experts can see it. However, your digital footprint is like a **permanent record**: once it is put down it is very difficult to remove.

Minding Mobile Devices

With our mobile phones we can talk, send messages and connect to the Internet from anywhere. Once online, we can use instant messaging applications to have text conversations with our friends. We can also take photos and videos and upload them to our social media accounts.

Handheld devices like phones or tablets contain a lot of our personal information so it's important to take care of them. **We need to protect them with a passcode in case they get stolen.** A passcode is like a password made up of numbers.

Hey Olivia, my mate wants your number.

We also need to be careful about who we give our **phone number** out to. Otherwise anyone could get hold of it.

Managing your Mobile

It's easy to click on something to download it to your phone, but is it always safe? Sometimes the file might be something that could harm your phone. At other times downloading it might cost money. Logging in to the Internet from your phone also costs money. For this reason **it is best to discuss using the Internet on your phone with your trusted adult.**

A girl at Olivia's school gave out her phone number to a friend of a friend and now she gets all sorts of unwanted messages. Olivia knows to **keep her phone number protected.**

Sorry — I only give it out to close friends.

My Phone is Missing!

If your mobile phone is lost or stolen it's best to talk to your trusted adult as soon as possible. They can help call the police and your mobile phone provider, and then make your social media accounts secure. This means changing all of your passwords. Doing this will prevent the thief accessing your accounts and pretending that they are you.

Awesome Internet

Ever wondered how to say 'hello' in Swedish, build your own kite, or take guitar lessons without leaving the house? The Internet can teach you how! **There are short videos online which can show you how to do everything,** from making toys to learning a new instrument.

Pronouncing a foreign word could not be easier. Just try typing 'hello in Swedish' into your search engine. Now click on 'Hallå' to hear how to say it. Simple! That's why the Internet is awesome – it is a great learning tool.

Chapter 3: Click and Connect

Emails and Viruses

In a few clicks we can communicate using social media, instant messaging and email. Email is like getting a letter through your letterbox in lightning-fast time. But just like junk mail through the letterbox, you may receive emails from people you don't know.

Called spam, these emails are often harmless. At other times, they may carry a virus that can harm your computer. Some may be from cyber strangers trying to make contact, or people wanting you to spend money. **It's always best to check a new email carefully before opening it.**

I don't know who this is from but it has the new game attached.

Sounds too good to be true - delete, delete, delete!

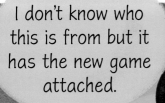

Like letters through your letterbox, spam emails can promise gifts and free goodies. Don't be fooled: click the 'spam' button. This deletes the email and stops more from the same address reaching your inbox.

Email Fakes

Some advertisers send out fake emails to millions of addresses hoping for a reply. If someone does reply, the advertiser knows that email address is real. Then they bombard that person with spam. It's best to follow a simple email rule: **if you don't know who an email is from, then delete it**.

VIRUS

FAKE EMAIL

SPAM

MALWARE

VIRUSES

ADVERTISEMENT

 ¿ STRANGER ?

Malware and Viruses

Viruses and malware are both types of software designed to harm your computer. They are often sent as a link or an email attachment. Sometimes these attachments are disguised to look like something you'd like, such as a free download. It's important never to open these emails and instead delete them straight away.

Meeting Social Media

Social media websites are like online clubs. Once you've joined you can share your news with other club members. Usually you do this on your 'wall', a place where you can post photos and videos and write a daily blog. Everyone in the club can do the same and comment on each other's posts. It's a great way of staying connected with friends.

But in a real-life club **you wouldn't share your news with somebody you didn't know.** Social media is the same.

Privacy Settings

When you first join a social media website you can select different privacy settings. This means you decide who sees your wall. The settings usually let you choose: 'only my friends', 'friends of friends', or 'everyone'. **It's best only to allow 'only my friends' access.** If someone you don't know invites you to be their friend, it is best not to accept. You can also block people. Your trusted adult can help you with these settings.

Tony1953 wants to join and read your new games blog.

Friends and Followers

Some people have lots of 'friends' on social media. But how many of those people do they actually chat with? **Isn't it better to have a few close friends to share things with, than many that you don't know well?**

Cyber Chatting

Having text conversations is a great way of chatting to friends in real time. With instant messaging applications we can chat from wherever we are: the bus, street or park. We can also have text conversations in online chat rooms. Chat rooms are forums where you can meet and talk to other kids from all over the world. We get to know these kids through their username, avatar and the things they like. **But how can we be sure they are who they say they are?**

Being Cyber Stranger Aware

In a chat room everybody is a stranger. But we need to keep an eye out for certain cyber strangers. These are people who may be overly keen to become online friends and are very interested in you. They may say they are the same age as you and seem to understand your problems. **But they may also be lying.**

IRONMAN21

LEGOBOY8

I think you should block him.

Because everyone has a username and avatar to chat online, we don't know who they are in real life. Some may be cyber strangers pretending to be children.

Olivia's Chat Room Choices

Kidzworld (www.kidzworld.com)
Kidscom.com (www.kidscom.com)

Sometimes, the cyber stranger may be an adult pretending to be a child. They may ask you to send pictures of yourself or to meet up. This is very dangerous. You should never arrange to meet someone you have met online unless your parents are involved. **If someone asks to meet, it is best to tell your trusted adult straight away.** This is also why it is important never to give away your personal information online (see page 17).

Posting Photos

It's easy and quick to upload photos and videos on social media. But it's also easy to forget that posting a photo might not be such a clever idea. It could hurt someone's feelings or **give away too much information** about ourselves, our friends or family.

One Picture is Worth 1,000 Words

Sam and Olivia take loads of photos at Maria's birthday party. Sam gets a brilliant shot of the birthday girl. But by posting the photo online is he giving too much information about Maria away? Look at the scene and see if you can spot **four** pieces of personal information that should remain private.

Once Shared, Forever Shared

The problem with posting photos on the Internet is that you can't control what happens to them. They can be copied and shared, and then they can appear anywhere. **Once something appears on the Internet it is almost impossible to delete it.** That's why it pays to think twice before uploading something – especially if it shows you or someone you know.

I'm going to put that up online.

Be careful Sam, you might be giving Maria's personal information away.

Awesome Internet

Did you ever wonder what it is like to be a schoolchild in Iceland? What is it like growing up in Mexico? Wonder no more – the Internet can tell you! There are websites about every different culture and country in the world. That's why the Internet is awesome: it celebrates our differences and similarities and shares them with everyone. Are you still wondering about what it is like to grow up in Mexico? Then check out this link:

www.kids-world-travel-guide.com/mexico-facts.html

Chapter 4: Searching the World Wide Web

All Sorts of Websites

Searching the World Wide Web is an exciting part of being online. This is how we discover our favourite websites and learn more about the things we like. Not all websites are suitable for kids though. Some are boring, others confusing, and some show yucky pictures we don't want to see. That's why your trusted adult is a good safe-searching friend.

Web Browsers

To search the World Wide Web we type what we are looking for into a program called a web browser. Safari, Chrome, Internet Explorer and Firefox are popular web browsers. You can put special filters on most web browsers to make them safe for kids. This means you won't come across adults'-only websites. Ask a trusted adult for help.

Upsetting Sites

If you see something that upsets you online, the simplest thing is to tell your trusted adult. They can help you block the website and make you feel better by talking about it.
Remember: you never have to look at something you don't want to online, even if your friends say it's cool. Just click out of it.

You never know what you'll come across online. That's why you should always have a trusted adult around when you're searching the World Wide Web.

29

Steering Straight in the Winding Web

Sometimes being online can be a bit crazy and chaotic. Windows can pop-up suddenly. Alerts can warn you about software updates. Adverts can flash in front of you. And invitations from people to become friends can come at any moment. Sometimes it's hard not to get hot and bothered! The main thing is to stay calm and not feel pressured to click on anything you're not sure about.

Sometimes it's hard to stay on a straight path when you are searching the web. You have to steer around pop-up windows, chat icons and adverts wherever you go.

SOFTWARE ALERT

SALE

Contests and Free Prizes

Have you ever had a pop-up window tell you that you've won a new iPhone or Playstation? Did it ask you to fill out some forms so your prize can be sent out to you? Don't be fooled! These are just ways of getting your details so advertisers can bombard you with spam. The simplest thing is to **never click on a pop-up window,** and if you do by accident, then click straight out again.

Installing Software

Have you ever tried to watch a sports match or music video and have an alert tell you that you need to update your software? Sometimes this is true: it is your computer telling you that it needs to download an update. At other times, it is someone trying to send you a virus or malware, or divert you to a different website. **The best thing is to ask your trusted adult when these alerts appear.**

Buy By Accident

It's easier than ever to buy things on the Internet. Many online stores save a computer user's details so they can purchase items with a single click. This can cause trouble if your whole family uses the same computer to go online. If this is the case, make sure you are extra careful. Sometimes games can ask you to buy an add-on that makes them more fun. Make sure always to say no to this, unless you are sure that they are free!

20% OFF!

Dangerous Downloads

The Internet is the perfect place to find music and films. Some websites let you stream music for free if you watch their adverts. YouTube is a website that lets you watch videos for free.

To download music and films onto your computer, tablet or phone you usually have to pay. However, there are also illegal websites which let you download the same files for free. Although lots of people use these websites you should not be one of them. If you are caught, you could get into serious trouble.

But it doesn't seem right to get a new film for free.

Don't worry – everyone's doing it!

Sam's friend has a copy of a new film that has just come out at cinemas. Now Sam can have his own copy for free. But should he accept it?

File Beware

Illegal music and film files are often of poor quality and can come with a **nasty surprise** attached. Sometimes, the files might have the correct name but instead turn out to be an advert or contain a virus. Because you have downloaded the file, your anti-virus software won't help. This could really mess up your computer, phone or tablet.

Why is it Illegal?

Most films, songs and books are copyrighted by law. A copyright means the creator of the work gets to say what people do with it. This means it is illegal to use it without the creator's permission. **Illegally downloading or sharing a copyrighted film, song or book over the Internet is called piracy.** Piracy is just another word for stealing and doing so is against the law.

Great Gaming

Online games are designed for fun and there are different ones for every device. You can play a single player game on your phone or tablet, or against dozens of opponents on your gaming console or computer. Playing a multiplayer game can be a bit like being on a social media website. Gamers can chat and offer tips. But online gamers are also like the number of games online – every one is different. **Some gamers can get nasty and others are not who they say they are.** Keep your cyber-stranger radar on when you are playing!

Ouch, what did I do to deserve that? I don't want to play anymore.

It's Just a Game

Sometimes gamers get very competitive. Some can say nasty things. This is never acceptable. If someone says something upsetting, take a screen shot of their comments as a record. Ask your trusted adult how to do this. Your trusted adult can also help report the comments to the website. Never reply to nasty comments.

Handles and Avatars

It's important to always choose an avatar picture and a handle (gaming username) when playing games online. Choose one that is different from the usernames you have on different websites. Remember to follow your rules about not giving out information about yourself (see page 13). Be careful if another player is very interested in you. Who knows who they really are?

THORHAMMER1, YOU'RE RUBBISH!

The Real World is Awesome

Have you ever sat down for a quick online game, just to find that hours have passed? It's easy to spend time in the world of the Internet – but **there's also a real world** happening. A simple way not to miss out is to give yourself a time limit for each online session. Set an alarm to make sure you stick to it.

Chapter 5: Being a Good Digital Citizen

Online Etiquette

Has someone ever said something mean to you in real life? Or written something nasty to you online? Both are equally hurtful. Sometimes computer users forget that they are talking to real people on social media, chat rooms or online games. They think it's ok to be rude or nasty – but it is not.

How we behave online should be no different from how we behave in the real world. This means **treating other people online as we would like to be treated ourselves.** We should be polite, respect others, and report anything we think is harmful. This is known as being a good digital citizen.

BUS STOP

Did you see the Brazil game last night? The goal was amazing!

It was good. I watched it with my dad.

OLIVIA JUST TOLD ME THE MATCH WAS GREAT. EVERYONE ELSE THINKS IT WAS RUBBISH. LOL.

What you say in the online world has the same effect as in the real world. Before posting a comment about someone, ask yourself: "Would I be happy saying this to his or her face?" If not, don't post it.

Online Etiquette

Etiquette means the rules for behaving well. Below are some guidelines to follow for good online etiquette:

- Always be polite and kind to others.
- Make sure you respect the opinions of others – even if you disagree with them.
- Never say anything mean to someone, even if you think they deserve it.
- Don't ever spread a nasty or rude message about someone else.
- Don't say anything online that you wouldn't want your parents to read.

Do you like my new trainers?

They're awesome. Let me take a photo.

THESE ARE SAM'S NEW TRAINERS. REALLY COOL

... NOT!

Send an Online Smile

Your online reputation is important. It's not only about avoiding saying bad things, it's also about saying good things. Posting **funny, kind and positive** comments online will make people smile and brighten up their day. This helps make the Internet a friendly, fun and exciting adventure for everyone.

Cyber Bullying

Cyber bullies and trolls are people who say nasty things and spread lies about others online. A cyber bully is often someone you know who has decided to pick on you. They could send you mean text messages or emails, or post nasty comments about you on social media. They could post embarrassing photos online that you don't want others to see, or give away your personal information.

The first thing to remember is that **cyber bullying can happen to anyone.** The next thing is to take some steps to stop it.

Beat the Bully

If you find yourself the victim of a cyber bully, these are some steps you can take to help:

- Never reply to a bully's messages, or it may encourage them.
- Tell your trusted adult what is happening and ask for their help.
- Take a screen shot of every nasty message as evidence.

What is a Troll?

A troll is a type of online bully who likes to target strangers instead of people they know. Trolls often lie quietly in wait in chat rooms before launching an attack. This usually involves arguing, swearing and saying nasty things about other users.

Often a troll has a mean-sounding screen name. The easiest way to deal with a troll is to ignore them. If they do not get any attention, trolls usually get bored and go away. However, you should report their comments to the website anyway.

Being the victim of cyber bullying is a big shock that can seem like a joke at first. It's important to take it seriously and seek help from your trusted adult straight away.

- Only answer your phone if it is a number or person you know.

- If you are being bullied on your social media account, block the bully and click on the 'report abuse' button.

- Tell your close friends what is happening. It is better to share than keep bullying a secret.

- Remember: it is not your fault you are being bullied!

39

Bullying Bystanders

Some cyber bullies encourage others to join in and pick on a victim together. This can involve spreading a bully's nasty messages and 'liking' the hurtful things they have said on social media. The bullies can even give out their victim's email address, phone number and social media information.

We're getting this kid Sam. I'll text you his number and email address.

Some bullies pressure others to join the bullying. This can be terribly upsetting if the victim is you. It can feel like the **whole world is against you** and there is nowhere to escape from the abuse. This is why it is important never to join in when somebody is being bullied, and instead try to stop it happening. Protecting ourselves and other people is a big part of being a good digital citizen.

Doxing Details

Doxing means to post someone's personal information online so others can bully them. Some bullies even hack into their victim's online accounts to find these details.

This is why it is important to protect your personal details and choose strong passwords for your social media accounts. This makes a bully's job difficult or can even prevent them from bullying you in the first place.

"This isn't right. I'm going to help Sam."

Victims of cyber bullying can feel alone and like no-one is on their side. For this reason, it's important to support these victims and show you think the bullying is wrong.

Don't Be a Bystander

A bystander is someone who watches something happening but does nothing to help. **When cyber bullying happens there are often many bystanders who take no notice.** They think it is none of their business or can't be bothered to try and stop it. When bystanders spread a cyber bully's nasty messages they become bullies too. Instead, offering support to a person that is being bullied or reporting the bully can make a huge difference.

Reporting Abuse

Being a good digital citizen means reporting cyber bullying or any other form of online abuse. Start by telling your trusted adult. There are also phone helplines just for kids that you can call (see page 47). Your conversation will be kept private if you want it to be.

If the cyber bullying is happening at your school, tell the head teacher. Your trusted adult or head teacher may then involve the police. All of these things will help stop cyber bullying and make the Internet a better, safer place for everyone.

Preventing Peer Pressure

Sometimes you may see your friends being mean to someone online. Several friends may be encouraging each other and forgetting that they are hurting someone else's feelings. If you see this happening, talk to your friends and remind them how upsetting their behaviour is. You can also explain the situation to your trusted adult for advice.

The head teacher wants to see you in her office, Ratfink17.

Uh-oh. How did you know my username?

Cyber bullying is a form of harassment and is taken seriously by the police. Many cyber bullies find they cannot hide in the online world for long.

Catching Cyber Crooks

All computer devices that go online have an Internet Protocol (IP) address. This is how other computers know where to send and collect their information. Your IP address is a bit like a fingerprint. This is how the police are able to trace people online and catch wrongdoers.

Awesome Internet

Does it ever seem like you are the only person in the world that likes the same stuff you do? Does it make you feel alone in the world? Well, you're wrong! There are many people who think the way you do. Just have a look on the Internet. You'll find loads of people that like the same stuff. That's why the Internet is awesome. It can make us feel good about ourselves and the things that we love.

The Online Quiz

Cyber Sam and Online Olivia now know how to avoid the dangers on the Internet. How about you? See how prepared you are by taking this quiz.

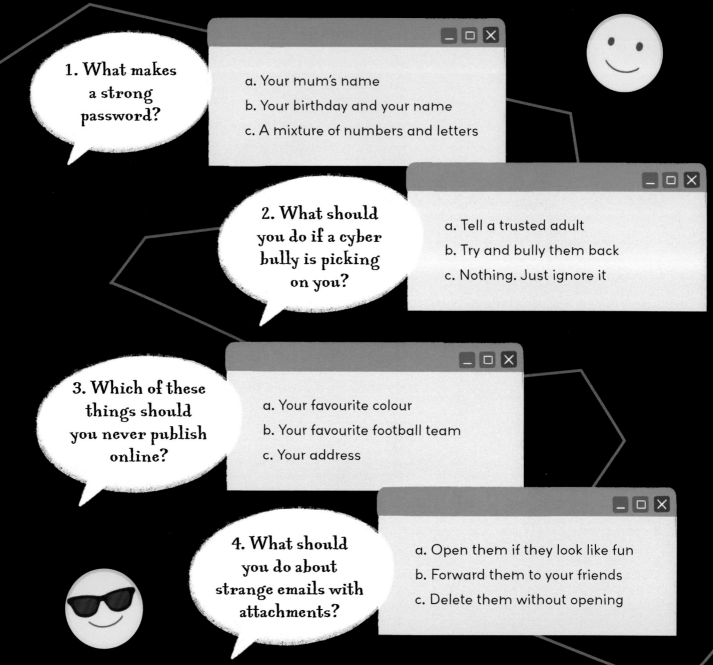

1. What makes a strong password?

a. Your mum's name

b. Your birthday and your name

c. A mixture of numbers and letters

2. What should you do if a cyber bully is picking on you?

a. Tell a trusted adult

b. Try and bully them back

c. Nothing. Just ignore it

3. Which of these things should you never publish online?

a. Your favourite colour

b. Your favourite football team

c. Your address

4. What should you do about strange emails with attachments?

a. Open them if they look like fun

b. Forward them to your friends

c. Delete them without opening

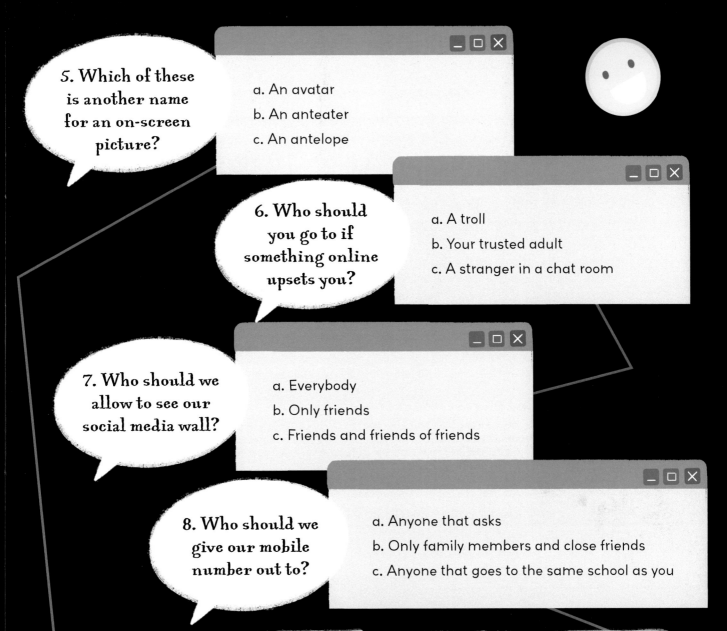

5. Which of these is another name for an on-screen picture?

a. An avatar
b. An anteater
c. An antelope

6. Who should you go to if something online upsets you?

a. A troll
b. Your trusted adult
c. A stranger in a chat room

7. Who should we allow to see our social media wall?

a. Everybody
b. Only friends
c. Friends and friends of friends

8. Who should we give our mobile number out to?

a. Anyone that asks
b. Only family members and close friends
c. Anyone that goes to the same school as you

How did you do?

Add up your score and see.

8/8: Congratulations. You are a smart, safe A1 Internet adventurer. Have fun online!
4-8: Well done, but have a look at the answers you got wrong to become an A-grader.
Less than 4: Good try but you may want to read the book again to get up to speed.

ANSWERS 1: c; 2: a; 3: c; 4: c; 5: a; 6: b; 7: b; 8: b

Glossary

Applications

Applications are programmes that do a particular job such as telling us the weather. Apps are shorter, simpler applications used on mobile devices.

Block

When you stop a computer user from sending you emails or looking at your social media pages.

Bully

Someone who deliberately makes another person feel bad by doing or saying nasty things.

Chat room

Website where people chat by typing text messages to each other.

Download

Transfer a file from the Internet onto your computer or device.

Favourites

A folder where you can store the addresses of your favourite websites.

Instant Messaging

A form of online chat that allows us to send text messages to each other in real time.

Malware

Computer programme designed to harm another person's computer.

Privacy Settings

The settings which allow you to choose who looks at your pages on social media.

Profile

The details you use about yourself for your online account, such as your username and avatar.

Report Abuse

A button found on many websites that allows you to report bullying or bad behaviour to the website organisers.

Search Engine

A website that we use to find information online.

Streaming

Watching a video or listening to music online without downloading it onto your computer device.

Trusted Adult

A parent, guardian, teacher or other adult who we trust to help us with the Internet.

Upload

Transfer a file from your computer device onto the Internet.

User name

The name you use instead of your own on an Internet account such as social media.

Wi-Fi

A wireless Internet connection.

Helpful Websites

The following websites offer further information about staying safe online.

Childline is a help phone line for children that you can call for advice at any time of day or night. Ring: 0800 1111. Childline's website also has advice about online bullying:

www.childline.org.uk/get-support/

Website dedicated to staying safe online:

www.safetynetkids.org.uk

A special online safety website for kids from 5–14 years old:

www.thinkuknow.co.uk

A website for online safety with special advice for primary and secondary children:

www.childnet.com/young-people

BBC online safety guide for kids:

www.bbc.com/bitesize/guides/z9p9kqt/revision/1

For readers in Australia

Kids Helpline is Australia's free, 24/7 phone and online counselling service for young people aged 5 to 25. Ring 1800 55 1800. On their website, go to the 'Tips and Info' section to get to advice for staying safe online:

kidshelpline.com.au

Books

Kids Get Coding: Staying Safe Online, Heather Lyons; Elizabeth Tweedale, Wayland 2016

Get Ahead in Computing: Computer Networks, Clive Gifford, Wayland 2016

Keep Yourself Safe: Being Safe Online, Honor Head, Franklin Watts, 2015

Teen Life Confidential: Texts, Tweets, Trolls and Teens, Anita Naik, Wayland 2014

Let's Read and Talk About: Internet Safety, Anne Rooney, Franklin Watts, 2014

Index

Dad says we shouldn't have our phones or computers with us at night. That way we get a good night's sleep without being disturbed. Goodnight!